What the L?

Finding Balance:
Creating and *Maintaining a New Mindset*

KeKe Chanel

NDJ Publishing

To Ryan

Thank you for letting me love you.
You have forever changed my life.

**Finding Balance:
Creating and Maintaining a New Mindset**

Introduction

*F*inding balance in our lives is essential to living our *best* life. It all begins with a common factor—a factor that many people lose sight of, or overlook altogether. Although balance aligns every area in our lives, pushing us into our purpose and destiny, a new mindset is one key to creating and maintaining the life we desire. Deciding to embrace change is another.

What the L is a step-by-step guide on what we should focus on to create and maintain a new mindset that can eventually produce a happier and healthier lifestyle.

Six L-words come to mind when I think about leading a more enriched and balanced life. It all begins with transforming our minds. When we change our minds, we change our lives.

These six L-words have played an important role in my life and I'm sure they will do the same for you when applied. You probably know them all anyway. I'm sure you do. They are words we hear every day which should make incorporating them into your life a breeze. Being mindful of these six words can open up endless possibilities for us all. We will become more insightful and appreciative. We will strive for more and stop settling for less.

Doing anything of significance in our lives requires cultivation. Cultivating our thoughts, feelings, emotions, etc. is essential to the way we live. Why? Because with cultivation comes manifestation. What is manifestation, one might ask? My definition of manifestation isn't like those you might find in the dictionary or on google. It's simple. Manifestation is experiencing the art of cultivation (preparation) for the things we desire;

something that comes to pass. Manifestation requires a new mindset. To develop a new mindset, we have to open our hearts to being accountable for our actions and internal guidance.

Internal guidance comes from within. It's when we step into a new thought process that unblocks and declutters our minds by adopting a new way of thinking. We think from a soulful and more mindful perspective instead of a physical one. Yet, we are also able to think realistically. Point being, the way we train our thinking produces and reflects in our everyday lives.

Throughout this book, I will explore six word-options. I will break them down for a better understanding of what is imperative in creating and maintaining a new mindset which, in turn, helps us create and maintain a balanced life—something we all desire and deserve.

Mindset matters.

The way we think breeds what we tend to focus on. Our thoughts trigger our emotions, feelings, and actions. Therefore, our reactions are stemmed from factors we can control if we understand how. We have to mind our thoughts to transform our perception.

Changing our perception develops a new sense of understanding, resulting in a new way of thinking. This realization brings me to the first L-word we should focus on to bring balance to our lives.

Listen:

To give attention with the ear; attend closely for the purpose of hearing; pay attention; heed; obey; to hear.

LISTEN

When we listen, we gain a better understanding—a broader perspective in every area of our life. We open ourselves to new possibilities, pushing us toward the life we desire and deserve. Listening is one of the first forms of communication we grasp as an infant. From the womb, we understand sounds, particularly the sound of our mother's voice or music. To listen is to learn or process information. Processing information is also called comprehension. We cannot comprehend anything without focus, intention, and practice.

To do anything well, we must mentally internalize it first. Holding on to valuable information gives us a sense of accomplishment, which creates fulfillment in our subconscious mind. What is the subconscious mind? It's a bank/well of stored data for everything. It stores your beliefs, life experiences, memories, skills, etc. Everything we've ever seen, done, or thought is stored in the subconscious mind. Subconsciously, we hold on to things we never realize—stuff that can block our paths to growth, success, knowledge, etc.

Let's use fear as an example. We can subconsciously retain the presence of fear whether we have overcome it or not. Facing fear is a pivotal process to personal growth and mindset. It remains buried inside our thoughts until we bring it to the forefront of our minds so that we can release it. It isn't until we tap into that part of our brain—the temporal lobe—that we become unstuck. The temporal lobe helps us integrate information from other senses. When we can do that, we are then able to let go of the things we hold on to unknowingly—the things that hold us back from reaching our full potential.

Unpacking mental baggage opens our minds. We then broaden our ability to grow—to transform ourselves from ordinary to extraordinary beings. Meaning, when we listen to comprehend versus listen to respond, we can hear with the intention to gain a better understanding which makes us mindful of our thoughts before expressing them. We tap into greater thinking and listening abilities that can push us into our next level.

Have you ever talked to someone who didn't pay attention—listen—to what you were saying? It's frustrating, right? The conversation doesn't go as we hope.

People often listen to what they want to hear, especially when they are interested in the topic of discussion. When it's something they don't care about or want to be a part of, they block it out or focus their attention on something else. This behavior leaves the other person feeling let down, guarded, or regretful.

Some people can stare you straight in the eyes, smile, and nod as you speak and not hear a word that comes out of your mouth. How? Because in most cases, subconsciously, their minds are telling them that they should be distracted. I'm not saying this is true for every time someone doesn't pay attention to what we say. I'm giving an example. We are all probably guilty of this at some point in our lives. But, when we know better, we do better. Right? That should be the goal.

Lack of empathy and compassion toward others are the culprits of such behavior. Most individuals don't appreciate others saving space for them until the gesture is no longer accessible. Holding space for others is one of the most selfless acts one can display. We shouldn't take this for granted. No one owes us anything. We should respect and appreciate them when they make us a priority. We cannot fully grip this concept until we become consciously aware by redirecting our thoughts to what's real versus what's not. In other words, to hear we must learn to listen. One cannot understand the concept of being a good and reciprocal listener until they focus their thoughts on doing so.

In today's world, entitlement and privilege have confused society to its very core. As stated, no one owes us anything. But, we do owe ourselves. That starts with finding perspective—a new perspective, in most instances. We owe it to ourselves to become the best version of ourselves. We shouldn't let anyone or anything keep us from achieving this act of personal growth.

Being self-absorbed has become the new normal in today's culture. Why? Because people don't like to listen, instead we love to hear ourselves talk, especially about ourselves. Gossip is a prime example. We deflect and project, stirring someone else's pot instead of tending to our own. This leaves us malnourished with our mind, body, and soul starving for something more fulfilling.

Contrary to popular belief, listening and hearing are two very different things. Listening deals with paying close attention and hearing deals with perception. They both play huge roles in the communication process, but we have to value the process of creating and maintaining an enriched life for either to work. It depends on our ability to understand, as well as perceive what is meant for us to gain.

To develop a new mindset, we have to listen.

We cannot complete one action without the other. To hear one must first listen and vice versa. Only through listening intentionally will one understand the concept of hearing. To hear is to truly comprehend the concept of what listening entails.

We have to listen to our voice of reason to understand the depth of it. Listening is the first stop on the train to protecting our mental health. To know what's happening mentally, emotionally, and physically, we have to listen to our bodies and our thoughts.

Being mindful is connected to how we listen from within ourselves and to others. Through mindfulness, we should reach what's called a **mindset shift** *eliminating all negative feelings, thoughts, emotions, patterns, and reactions.* **Listen** is the first, yet, the most important *L-word* to help us find balance in our lives. When we can hold stimulating conversations, acquire and comprehend valuable information, and many other benefits, we become unstoppable. How? We renew our minds—change the way we think.

Mindset is hard work. It takes time, effort, discipline, and depends on each person deciding to evolve. A new mindset is a driving force behind our ability to change.

Daily practice is required.

When we listen, we clasp onto the next L-word without compromise. We are well on our way to personal growth by the renewing of our minds.

$\mathscr{L}$earn:

To acquire knowledge of or skill in by study, instruction, or experience; to become informed of or acquainted with; to memorize, to gain by example or the like.

LEARN

*E*quipping ourselves with knowledge and understanding are the best forms of the next *L-word* I want to talk about.

When we have a desire to **learn**, our minds expand, accepting new and unlimited prospects for our lives. Our lifestyles change. We become confident, focused, and optimistic. We experience a total mindset shift. I gave you the definition of a *mindset shift* in the previous chapter.

Learning inspires us to create and maintain balance in our lives for a happier and healthier life. It sharpens our minds and pushes us to level up. It's a known fact that when we know about a particular skill or topic, we speak passionately and boldly about it with others. People glean from us. They trust us to know what we're talking about, to guide them, and to impact them in some way or another.

We inspire, motivate, and challenge others to study, explore, and familiarize themselves with their crafts or whatever it is that they're passionate about.

Learning new things daily strengthens our minds. When our minds are sharp, our thoughts are positive; therefore, we generate and release positive energy to anyone around us including ourselves. We become what we think because our thoughts produce our reality. Acquiring knowledge can be empowering to individuals because it helps them to make more informed choices and/or broadens their view of the world.

To learn is to acquire something new. In most cases learning is a personal decision, but, there are instances in which learning disabilities can block one's ability to retain knowledge. Consequently, learning is a self-inflicted process that we must yearn for to accomplish. Why take someone else's word when you are fully capable of researching and learning for yourself? However, there are numerous ways to learn, and one is not always aware that they are learning. Still, the desire is there. For example, children pick up social and verbal cues from those around them. Are they always aware that they are learning how to navigate the world simply by observing? No, but there is still a jolt within them to learn things by trying something new. Independence produces growth personally and mentally.

Learning spawns determination, consistency, empowerment, and ultimately, purpose. To find our purpose, we have to discover our passions (likes/dislikes). Through balance, we embody intention. How? By knowing what we want and acting accordingly. An intention is a goal or something one hopes to accomplish. Taking on an intentional mindset brings balance which produces a structured lifestyle. When we focus on achieving a certain goal, we set our intentions in a positive and open way to achieve said goal(s).

Without the will to learn we become stagnant, trapped, and ordinary when we are meant for greater. Listen. We were not put here to stay comfortable in our lives when there is so much more for us. It's our responsibility, our choice, to live the best life that we can. When we learn, we raise the bar and set the tone for the life we wish to live. How? We not only talk about it, but we also act upon it. We take initiative. Our minds are clearer and ready to push ourselves to the next level.

If something doesn't challenge us, we aren't thinking big enough. When it doesn't make us uncertain or afraid, we haven't tapped into our full potential. Anything worth having, means getting out of our comfort zones. Being comfortable isn't something we should become accustomed to. If we are not uncomfortable at some point in our lives, we forfeit our advancement. And the uncomfortability I'm referring to does not involve placing oneself in a harmful or unjust situation and remaining there for the sake of progress. Don't be uncomfortable for the sake of being uncomfortable. That's not smart thinking.

I'm referring to personal growth. Nothing good lasts being inside our comfort zone. How will we achieve greater becoming complacent? We won't.

Growth comes with discomfort. Remember that the next time you experience an uneasy feeling about doing something new and exciting. The reward is greater when we cross the finish line, but it's the journey during the race that's most rewarding. Have a greater appreciation for tearing down any comfort zones to be set free. It is essential in how we move forward to the next phase of our lives.

Learn to grow. Learn to step away from your comfort zones. Learn to embrace change and accept new things. Learn to listen. Find balance. Create the life you want and deserve by renewing your mind with a new mindset.

When we become better, it reflects and radiates to everything and everyone around us. We also look better and feel better when we achieve the goals we set for ourselves. Our energy becomes a positive influence, making the world a brighter place.

Recently, I stepped out of my comfort zone and started my own talk show. It has been amazing! I learned to get out of my own way. There is no turning back for me now. Once I decided that I wanted more in my life, I wasn't as afraid. I didn't worry about the number of people who would watch or want to be a guest. I decided to do it for me—to further operate into my purpose. And you know what happened? My show is a success and I'm booked until next year. There is no turning back.

Be a light in not just your own life but those around you by learning to create and maintain a balanced life through a new mindset.

The people who are meant to come along with you will. Don't focus on anyone else.

Leap:

To spring through the air from one point or position to another; to jump; to move or act quickly or suddenly; to pass, come, rise.

LEAP

I listened to a training webinar a few weeks ago with world-renowned motivational speaker Lisa Nichols. If you don't know who Lisa Nichols is, look her up. She's awesome. Lisa's personal testimony will change your life.

Lisa said something profound during the webinar that resonated with me on a scale I've never allowed myself to acknowledge. It was truly an *ah-ha* moment.

When was your last *ah-ha* moment?

What are ah-ha moments? These are moments that pack a powerful, mental punch that helps us see things clearer. They are moments that profoundly transform our minds. *Ah-ha* moments are far and few in between, so whenever you encounter them, pay close attention. Write them down. Meditate and acknowledge them. You never know if or when you will get another. And, you will know when you experience one.

Ah-ha moments hit differently. They elevate our way of thinking. They give us just the right *push* to leap. Their insight grabs our attention and expands our mentality by giving us the desire to strive for more and the courage, motivation, and insight to get up if knocked down.

During the webinar, Lisa said, *"One of three things will happen when you leap. Even if you leap afraid: You'll fly and everything will be alright, you'll fall and land on something soft, and everything will be alright, or you'll fall and land on something really hard, and it'll hurt...and still, you'll be alright."*

This brings me to the next *L-word*: **leap.**

Life happens whether we are prepared for it or not. It stops for no one. To somewhat be ready for disappointments and distractions, we have to develop our leap dynamic. One way to overcome, empower, and transform is to leap.

Taking chances is crucial in our relationships, careers, businesses, education, etc. We have to put ourselves out there by leaping toward something greater. Otherwise, we cheat ourselves when it comes to our successes.

If you're at a stage in your life where you feel stuck and ready for elevation, I challenge you to do it—whatever *it* is, today. However, the 'whatever' *I*'m referring to should not be harmful to oneself or others. Leap without fear, meaning: Do it even if you are fearful of failing. This builds character.

Never give in to that fear. Don't allow obstacles or people who don't see your vision the way you do to keep you from leaping into your destiny. Leap! You never know what's ahead until you move forward. And sometimes, that might require you to take a few steps back to redefine your intention. If you don't know how just take baby steps. Leap small until you are ready to leap big. The point is to do it. Even if it's done while afraid, at least try.

What harm can it do?

You will either become a better person: spouse, parent, friend, employee, business owner, sibling, etc. Or, you will learn from your mistakes, listen along the journey, and leap harder the next time. What do you have to lose? Nothing, so leap! Leap like your life depends on it because, in all actuality, it does.

It's not until we get out of our own way that we flourish. As humans, we tend to overthink a lot. We cancel out positive outcomes by holding on to the *'coulda, woulda, shoulda's.'*

Self-sabotage doesn't get us anywhere. If anything, it keeps us stuck, too afraid to take chances. We become roadblocks without realizing that it's us all along standing between us and our destiny. It isn't until we change our mindset that we become aware of this subconscious nature we don't know how to let go. Then, and only then, can we leap without worrying about a safety net. When we can do that, we can truly enjoy the fullness of a balanced life!

_L_augh:

To express mirth, pleasure, derision, or to produce a sound resembling human laughter; to experience the emotion; vocal expulsion of air from the lungs that can range from a loud burst of sound to a series of chuckles; amusement; make fun of.

L-word#4

LAUGH

*W*e've all heard the saying, *'Laughter is good for the soul.'* I couldn't agree more. I, personally, know this statement to be true. Ask yourself this important question.

How often do you **laugh**?

Your answer should be simple. Why? Because everyone should laugh at least once a day to experience the joy of happiness. If not, there lies the problem. You don't laugh as you should. Make a conscious effort to do it more.

Every chance I get, I find humor in life. I laugh and mean it. I laugh as if today is my last day on earth and I want to feel good.

Did you know that laughter is a form of therapy dating back to the 1970s for pain and stress according to New Skills Academy: Mindfulness Certification Program?

People, who laugh more, live better and healthier lives. They are less stressed and fight off illnesses quicker than those who don't seek humor in basic everyday routines. People who laugh more are youthful, have positive attitudes, and live life with purpose.

Once we get out of the need to take ourselves so seriously, we tap into our truest potential of becoming the best version of ourselves. We experience that **mindset shift** I spoke of earlier.

When we take things too seriously, we tend to lose ourselves a little bit each day. We become susceptible to illnesses and diseases. We take on nervous energy and a pessimistic attitude, resulting in anxiety and depression. We forget to laugh and become lost in reality—our counterfeit perception of it. Counterfeit perception meaning: that people tend to view the world more negatively than they ought to. Everything and everyone upset us. We hold on to negativity and irritability, producing toxins in our bodies which may cause insomnia and weight gain, or even incurable illnesses.

To laugh is to let go, to release emotion. To see the world through a new mindset forms a better quality of life that's pleasing to our bodies and our minds. We bask in the little things and shake the bad ones off. We start fresh. We mind our thoughts. We free ourselves from mental and emotional attacks.

I'm thankful for my family and friends. They keep me laughing, and I do my best to return the gesture. To laugh is a beautiful distraction to the trials and tribulations of life. Those trials and tribulations will come.

Do you have someone who makes you laugh? If not, I suggest you reevaluate your social network. Being uptight isn't anything to brag about or strive to portray. The people around us should inspire us, motivate us—and, darn it, make us laugh!

My brother is one of the people I can always count on to make me laugh no matter how bad my day has gone, or whether I want to or not. Sometimes, all he has to do is FaceTime me and when we see each other, we burst into laughter for no apparent reason.

I can also always count on my Auntie Mary to bring bouts of stomach and cheek pain from laughing too hard at what comes out of her mouth. She doesn't care. Her goal is to make you laugh and it's always fulfilled. I'm smiling just thinking about some of the things she's said over the years. I love and appreciate her presence in my life.

My cousin Doc is another person I can count on to make me hold my side from laughing. He wit is outstanding, mixed with his Southern accent that I love so much. He really should have a show. People would cancel plans to watch just to hear what he says. My cousin Do is a bright light in my life and I cherish him for that. We laugh and boy do we do it well whenever we link up.

To laugh—to freely laugh—is to let down your guards or inhibitions. Feel it deep within, let it carry you into a new headspace. Embrace each laugh with a new desire, a desire for something more in your life. When we don't find humor and let it grab hold of us, we cheat ourselves out of priceless moments. Instead of appreciating them, we speed through them without a second thought, missing their importance and value.

Laugh the pain away. Laugh when you're happy or even when you're sad. Laugh to keep from doing or saying something you cannot take back. Through it all, laugh.

Sure, there will be plenty of times when all you want to do is cry, have a pity-party, or close everyone out. Don't. Life isn't designed to be sunshine and rainbows all the time. Storms will come. Find the silver lining and allow laughter to cleanse your mind and body.

Then, save space for yourself—schedule some 'me' time—so that you can heal. Making time for self-care is essential. It keeps us in a healthy mental place. It keeps us looking good and feeling good on the inside as well as the outside.

Set your mindset to positive thinking and reap the benefits. People will notice because guess what? They're always watching. Give them something to see. Use your laughter to help change the world, starting first, with your environment. Laughter is transmittable. Do it as much as you can, as often as you can. What harm can it do?

Love:

Passionate affection for another person; a feeling of warm personal attachment or deep affection; desire; beloved person; to have love or affection for; a strong liking for; take pleasure in, to need or require.

Love

Have you ever noticed the beauty of the sky at sunset? The gentle colors of orange, purple, and pink after a lovely sunny day, it can simply take your breath away in a way that's so pleasing it leaves you speechless. You bask in the imagery, feeling warm inside. You may even be too afraid to close your eyes and embed the scene into your mind for fear that you'll miss any moment of its divine nature. The sensation of the experience seems to reach the depths of your consciousness, sealing the moment there forever. This is what I think of when I reflect on the next L-word: **love**.

Becoming a parent is another example. When you become a parent, you instantly fall in love with the idea of having another person to take care of and protect—someone who will fill your life with purpose. When you feel the child growing inside you, you know without a doubt that you will do everything in your power to stay healthy to birth a happy baby into this world. Even if you don't physically give birth to a child, and that child comes into your life, you love that child with your whole heart. You ponder the thought of having someone to love who will love you unconditionally, forever.

Being a mother is my greatest joy, greatest accomplishment, and greatest treasure. It's a job I don't take lightly, and one that will take precedence over everything in my life. My children are my world. They make my life meaningful—better. They are the epitome of love.

Love drives life.

To lead a life without love is like eating mud off of porcelain china. It doesn't make sense. Stop allowing anything or anyone to keep you from opening yourself up to experience the abundance of love.

To love is to endure the precious power of belonging, nurturing, being true to oneself. The influence of love is everlasting and unconditional.

Consequently, we should exemplify this emotion to ourselves and those around us every single day we are blessed to see. It shouldn't matter if we know each other or not. With love comes compassion and empathy for all mankind. In a world where hate is the driving force behind ignorance, why not turn to the one thing that keeps peace and balance—love. There's nothing to lose by choosing love. Two things will happen. One, we bask in something beyond our imagination, or two, we learn from the experience. Either way, we become a better person by opening ourselves up to giving and receiving love.

Expressing love should bring us joy, peace, comfort, and good health. I don't know about you, but when I spread love, I go all in. I love hard and want everyone around me to reap the fullness of it.

Love is remarkable. It makes us see life through more than tunnel vision, accepting the ups with the downs, learning and growing.

Take a journey with me…

Do you remember the first time you felt the presence of love in your life? What did it feel like? Who did it involve? (Write down your answers and reflect on them.)

____

____

These are questions we should ask
ourselves when we forget the radiance
of what love is for us.

A person in love glows differently.
They stand out. They smile and
personify confidence. They look
good, feel good, and expect nothing
but good in their life. Their mindset is
clear, open, positive, and impactful.
People want to know their secret. But
there isn't one. It's simple. They
embrace love, experiencing the
fullness of it without compromise.
Now, this doesn't make a person blind

to the harshness of life, they simply handle those instances in a different nature. No, love doesn't keep bad things from happening. We would be foolish to think that. But, love helps make dealing with certain things more tolerable.

Love can conquer fear. Love can challenge comfort. Love can destroy hate, tumble pride, and shatter negativity when one operates in love despite the opposite abounding in the world.

The best gift we can give ourselves is self-love. The best gift we can give anyone else is love.

To truly love anything starts from within. Loving ourselves first makes it easier to love others. We have to make a conscious decision to spread love everywhere we go, to everyone and everything that we encounter. Giving love isn't always easy, yet, necessary in our journey of personal growth.

How do we move on from any negative thought, feeling, or action to let love drive our reactions?

By letting go—letting go of any hurt, pain, anger, disappointment, resentment, failure, stress, worry, etc. Anything that's damaging mentally, that causes us to falter the concept to be loving in our lives, we must decide to let go and embrace a new mindset.

Love is the catalyst for the last L-word. The two go hand-in-hand. If one is lacking, the balance of life becomes a playground for chaos—unnecessary drama no one wants.

Live:

To have life; be alive; to maintain or support one's existence; to provide for oneself; to pass life in a specified manner; to direct or regulate one's life; to cohabit; be capable of vital functions; to continue in existence, operation, memory, etc.

LIVE

I believe that this last L-word is by far the most important one to consider on our quest to find balance in our life. It rhymes with, give. We have to give ourselves permission to demonstrate this word.

We often go through life existing instead of living as our best selves. I know you're probably tired of hearing the phrase 'L*ive your best life,'* but it's not overrated. We don't say it enough, in my opinion.

To **live** is to pursue, push forth, progress. It's better than the alternative, right? It most certainly is!

Tomorrow isn't promised and today is an unknown journey. Still, we must be mindful of our pursuit of leading a balanced life. When we are intent on living happy and healthy lives, we make a strong effort to fulfill said desire. We consider all opportunities and embrace the endless possibilities that life can bring. We stop stressing over the things we cannot change and focus on the things we have control over. We worry less and pray more. We change our mindset, which triggers a ripple effect, opening us up to one great thing after another.

Our will for knowledge and developing new skills heightens. We latch on to meeting new people, allowing those people to help us become a better person. If not, we are still able to carry on finding those who are meant to walk beside us.

Letting others teach us is another way to heighten personal growth to live as our best selves. Letting go of anything holding us back is pivotal if we want to take our lives to the next level. Living in each moment, breathing them in, exhaling doubt is the blueprint for what a successful life looks and feels like. Why? We don't allow doubt, fear, or naysayers to get inside our heads and keep us from reaching our full potential. We change our circle by changing our mindset. We can then, and only then, get out of our own way. And when we can get out of our own way, we don't allow anyone or anything to block our path.

We *leap* into fear. We *listen* intentionally. We *laugh* and *learn* with a wonderful zeal that brightens the minds and fuels our bodies. We operate in **love**, letting it inspire and motivate us to be better today than what we were yesterday. We simply **live** a more pleasing, rewarding, and balanced life.

Our desire not only to survive, but to thrive becomes evident in our careers, families, relationships, etc. We communicate our needs. We stop settling. We are mindful of each moment, and strive to treat others the way we want to be treated. We live.

Incorporating these six simple L-words: *listen, learn, leap, laugh, love,* and *live* will change every area in our lives. It won't happen overnight, but just like with anything else, through practice and persistence, we will reach the ultimate goal of a new mindset.

I challenge you, yes you, dear reader, to look within and decide today, what kind of life you want to have. Remember that an open mind is a renewed mind. The choice is yours.

Life isn't promised. It can end without warning. What we do while we are here is our choice. Would you rather smile and be happy or become a resident of misery's hotel?

To live, you have to decide to do just that. It doesn't require lots of money or friends or education. Living is a state of mind. It takes commitment, determination, and effort. Sometimes we make things harder than it is. We overthink the small stuff and second-guess the things we know that aren't good for us.

Don't treat your life like an exam.

Change your mind and change your life. Take one day at a time. There's no rush in the process of personal growth. As long as you remain intentional in your pursuit toward a new mindset, everything will fall exactly as they should when they should.

But also, ask yourself this important question.

What kind of life will you make for yourself?

I implore each of you to think long and hard on this question before you answer it. It will change your life in the most amazing and rewarding way.

<u>Summary</u>

Anything worth having requires work. Incorporating these six L-words into our daily routines will manifest a new way of thinking. We are what we think. Changing our thoughts changes the way we see and handle the curveballs life throws at us.

Here are six tips to remember:

1. *Listen* to your inner voice. More often than not, our intuition won't steer us in the wrong direction. When we listen, we hear the important factors that make us better

people and bring balance to our lives.

2. *Learn* to get out of the way. Becoming an obstacle does nothing positive when it comes to conquering our fears so that we can create and maintain a new mindset.

3. *Leap* without worrying about a safety net. Embrace boldness.

4. *Laugh* as often as you can.

5. *Love* the life that you have. If you don't like it, do something to change it.

6. Live. It's that simple!

Following these six tips will have a positive impact on your life. Take a chance on yourself and watch what happens.

Here are some important questions to ask yourself to determine if you're operating in a positive mindset for a balanced life:

- Am I happy with my life at this present moment?
- In what ways can my life improve?
- Am I applying the six mentioned L-words in this book to my current life?
- What can I do to include these words in my daily routine?
- Am I mindful of my way of thinking?

- How can I become more mindful in my life?

- Have I ever experienced a mindset shift?

- How/When?

- What did my mindset shift feel like? Does my life reflect the shift?

- Am I truly living my best life?

Write your answers:

____

____

____

____

____

____

____

About the Author:

KeKe Chanel is a certified life coach, specializing in personal growth and mindset. She is an award-winning author of suspense fiction who has penned 17 books. KeKe is the founder and owner of P.U.S.H Life Coaching LLC in Louisiana.

When KeKe isn't working as a writing coach, coaching others in fulfilling their dream of becoming a published author, she is blogging, reading books, spending time with family and friends, and enjoying life.

KeKe is also the host of Kickin' It With KeKe a live online talk show on Instagram every Monday at 8 pm CST.

For more information about Author KeKe Chanel visit her website:
www.thekekechanel.com.

* 9 7 9 8 6 9 0 0 1 0 5 0 8 *